PUBLIC SPEAKING: BECOME MAGNETIC PUBLIC SPEAKER

PUBLIC SPEAKING PRACTICAL GUIDE FOR BECOMING A MAGNETIC SPEAKER FOR GLOBAL IMPACT, INFLUENCE & EXPONENTIAL INCOME.

AUTHOR NAYAN CHAUDHARY

Made with ♥ on the Notion Press Platform
www.notionpress.com

ACKNOWLEDGEMENT

"The quality of your life is based on your quality decisions". At every step, we need to make decisions. It's great that you decided to grab this book to take your life to the next level. I've pretty much finished this book in less than 48 hours, but it wouldn't be possible without the support of **my loved ones and team.** I want to express my gratitude to **my mentees** who prompted me to write this book on public speaking since they enjoyed & got massive value from my first book on advanced communication skills. Your support means the world to me.

Here, I want to specifically thank the three most amazing men in my life...

My teacher **Mr Rajesh Patil sir,** he believed in me when nobody does, he showed me the direction & helped me to get courage, confidence and faith in myself.

Special thanks to **Mr Kunj Channe**(founder of SCDR pvt ltd) for helping me to write the book and to present the book in the most persuasive way.

I am thankful to my lovely brother **Rohit Chaudhary** for being with me from the beginning of my public speaking journey.

I am super excited to see a massive transformation in your speaking skills.

Contents

Contents

Unlock Free Bonuses

To unlock free bonuses all you need to do is, take your photo with the book and share it with me(on WhatsApp at +91 96049-01971).

Bonus 1:

Get a Public Speaking skills course to become a magnetic speaker. Worth INR 2,000 for FREE.

Bonus 2:

Life-changing E-books to help you become the best version of yourself. - Worth INR 2,000 for FREE.

Bonus 3:

Get the opportunity to attend LIVE upcoming workshops on public speaking skills.- Priceless

UNLOCK FREE PRIZES NOW!

Do You Want Author Nayan To Mentor You?

She offers various services to help you reach your full potential and develop your public speaking skills. You can select any of these alternatives if you want her mentorship.

1-1 MENTORSHIP FOR PUBLIC SPEAKING SKILLS

This two-month intense program is for you if you're searching for personalized speaking coaching to advance your public speaking abilities. WhatsApp her at +91 96049-01971 for further information.

GROUP SESSIONS

She offers group coaching to businesses, organizations, and institutions to help them speak effectively and courageously on stage. You can call her for both free and paid group sessions for your audience.

LARGE WORKSHOPS

Besides, she provides coaching for enterprises and organizations that would continue for at least five days. Where thousands of spectators would be there. Therefore, she is available if you need her for comprehensive workshops. Additionally, she runs her own independent projects, like

60 DAYS SOCIAL SKILL CHALLENGE

Where you get 60 days of training for your social skills. The unique aspect of this program is that you receive personalized feedback, hand-holding support, and weekly live workshops from Author Nayan to help you transform.

PUBLIC SPEAKING TRAINING

During this one-month training course, she will assist you in developing your overall public speaking abilities and helping you to become a fearless and confident public speaker.

STARTING YOUR COACHING BUSINESS

As you know that Author Nayan is an international public speaking mentor, Founder & CEO of ANC transformation. She is assisting individuals in more than 50 different nations. If you are just starting out and uncertain about how to go with your coaching career and want more customers, more speaking engagements, and more revenue, take advantage of her guidance. Personal mentoring is provided here.

To join any of these programs or to invite her to train your audience, team, or students, send her a WhatsApp message at +91 96049-01971.

CHAPTER ONE

5 REASONS WHY YOU MUST MASTER PUBLIC SPEAKING SKILLS

There was a time when I was not good at public speaking skills. Every time I tried to speak in front of a group of people, I would get extremely nervous and my mind would go blank. As a result, I lost out on a lot of opportunities that could have helped me further in my career.

I was always present at events, despite because I wasn't good at public speaking, people weren't aware of me or my work. I felt invisible and it was frustrating. I knew I had to do something to change the situation, so I decided to start learning more about public speaking.

I read books, watched videos, attended workshops on the subject & started observing speakers. I practiced my speeches over and over again until I felt more confident. And finally, after a lot of hard work, I started to see results.

People began to take notice of me and my work. I started getting invited to give talks and presentations. Slowly but surely, I became better and better at public speaking.

Today, I'm proud to say that I've mastered the art of public speaking, I am helping people across the world i.e 50+ countries. I'm grateful that I made the decision to learn more about it, because it has truly changed my life for the better.

> "*"Don't look for perfection; look for progress. There is always room for improvement in everything you do."*"

Let me share with you why public speaking is extremely important.

1. YOU GET MORE RECOGNITION

People will work with you when you can boldly and fearlessly communicate your ideas because they have seen you perform on stage, this increases their level of trust in you. Here hundreds of people are watching you and they are on your side. Ensure that people are familiar with you. They ought to be aware of what you do and how, in your area of expertise, you can assist them.

2. YOU ACHIEVE MORE IN LESS TIME

When you can speak in front of a large audience and convey your thoughts and opinions, you can accomplish more in less time. You can reach a huge audience in just one talk instead of taking days or months to do it.

"*"Action is the foundational key to all success."- Picasso*"

3. YOU CREATE LOTS OF OPPORTUNITIES

People want to work with you once they know & trust you, therefore you generate a lot of opportunities since you have established your authority and credibility in the industry. However, this can only happen when we present ourselves to the public.

4. YOU DEVELOP YOUR PERSONAL BRAND

People will start to recognise you by your face, your name and your brand, once you begin expressing yourself freely in front of a broader audience. As a consequence, your personal brand will start to grow and your personal and professional lives will advance.

Every person needs to create a personal brand for themselves. No matter what your area of expertise is, you can take steps to ensure that people associate you with your field.

5. YOU GENERATE LOTS OF MONEY

People will recognise you when they know you, and you will accomplish more in less time. You will start creating a lot of opportunities for yourself, which will help you build a strong personal brand and make tons of money.

> "*"You see, in life, lots of people know what to do, but few people actually do what they know. Knowing is not enough! You must take action."*
> *-Tony Robbins*"

Now you must have realised the power of public speaking. It is a powerful skill to master to grow in personal and professional life. It will help you to go to the next level.

Let's face it nothing comes for free, we have to pay the price to perfect it, you must dedicate hours, days, and even months, but trust me, it will be worthwhile.

Excuses never get you anywhere; only action does!

There will always be a reason why now isn't the right time, and that's the problem! Therefore, we must make achieving our goals for life a MUST!!!

When we make it a MUST, we find a way. And that is when the magic happens! Have full confidence that you will achieve all of your dreams. We don't know how long we are here for, so let's love every minute of it!

Always remember life is in the PRESENT; embrace it, love it, and enjoy every moment of your life. Heal the past pain, get rid of limiting beliefs, and learn new skills. Learn to love yourself and your life, move towards your big Desire.

An exercise that must be done

If you are unable to take action then just announce it(your goal) to the world or with your close ones, set a deadline. This helps you to be accountable. Therefore you will take the steps for your beautiful life.

CHALLENGE FOR YOU

1. What is your reasons to master public speaking skills (Write Your Why below).

____

____

____

____

____

2. Share your next plan with the world (to prevent procrastination).

____

____

____

____

CHAPTER TWO

GET EXTREME MOTIVATION TO PRACTICE SPEAKING SKILLS

Do you find that every time you try to practise your speaking skills, you lose motivation because of fear or pushing your limits and are unable to continue for a longer period?

I experienced the same difficulty. I know it is challenging and it gives you both mental and physical pain. However, the outcomes are excellent. To ensure a successful future, we must push ourselves to the utmost. Here, I'll tell you what I did to drive myself to stop procrastinating & start working on my speaking skills, you can also implement the same.

"Do the difficult things while they are easy and do the great things while

they are small. A journey of a thousand miles begins with a single step". – Lao Tzu

Even a large goal is more approachable if you break it down into smaller ones and just get started.

Practising your public speaking skills can be motivational if you follow these tips:

1. SET CLEAR GOALS

Determine your goals for public speaking and use those as inspiration to keep practising. Whether you want to improve your confidence, build your professional profile, or make a difference in your society, having a clear goal in mind can be a powerful motivator.

> ***“"If you don’t know where you are going, you will probably end up somewhere else." –Lawrence J. Peter”***

2. SET YOUR LONG-TERM AND SHORT-TERM MOTIVATIONS

Avoid procrastination by setting long-term and short-term motivation.

Long term motivations

- You hope to provide your family the life they deserve by living in the home of their dreams.
- You want financial freedom.
- You want to go on holiday to different countries.
- You want to work for uncertainty like health challenges or crises.
- You desire to support individuals financially or with your knowledge and abilities.
- You want to create an impact in society.

In my case, my long-term objective is to help 1 million people reach their greatest potential by empowering them to master their life through social and public speaking skills and by improving themselves until 2030.

Make a list of long-term motivations which will motivate you to take action

Short term motivations

Let's talk about the short-term drive that stimulates you to take action. You'll be inspired right away by these inspirations.

- Change your physiology, smile, laugh or think about some positive memory, or funny memory, and get in a good mood.
- Promise yourself a treat at the end of the task
- You can listen to energetic positive music that will raise your mood and get you pumped up.
- Picture yourself having the benefit of your task.
- Take a break to refresh yourself.
- Give yourself a Pep talk to get motivated.
- Google biographies of people you look up to.
- Declutter your work environment.
- Create a to-do list and break your task into smaller tasks.

- Change location.
- Get a coach.
- Post what you are working on, on social media.

Keep both long-term and short-term motivation in mind if you want to stop procrastinating.

3. FIND A MENTOR

Connect with someone who has experience and expertise in public speaking, and learn from their experiences. Having a mentor can provide inspiration and guidance as you work to improve your skills.

> ***"“A mentor is someone who allows you to see the hope inside yourself.” — Oprah Winfrey"***

I have already helped more than 15,000 corporate professionals and business leaders from 50+ countries to speak confidently and fearlessly from the stage. I can be your mentor to help you find your inner speaker.

> ***"The secret of getting ahead is getting started. – Mark Twain"***

Blanco

CHALLENGE FOR YOU

1. Which specific area of public speaking do you want to strengthen?

____

2. Set your long-term and short-term motivations.

CHAPTER THREE

9 MYTHS OF PUBLIC SPEAKING

More people fear public speaking than they do death. Several myths about public speaking exist, each of which can serve as a strong justification for not attempting it. But the truth is we all are capable of more than we know. Erase these 9 public-speaking myths from your mind, and you'll rapidly improve your confidence.

MYTH #1. PUBLIC SPEAKING IS AN INBORN TALENT

> ***"Great speakers are not born, they're trained ~ Dale Carnegie"***

Good speakers are not born, they are made by their constant efforts and practice. It can be learned and improved with practice, preparation, and feedback.

They may have been given the opportunity to develop a set of skills that support good public speaking early on in life & then encouraged to work on those skills continuously. They became comfortable with the idea of public speaking long before you knew about them, so they had a chance to get good at it at a younger age. Remember "No speakers are born only babies are born"

MYTH #2. INTROVERTS CAN'T BE GOOD PUBLIC SPEAKERS

Even though I am an introverted person, I have mastered the ability to switch to speaking mode whenever necessary. It was challenging at first, but with practice and repetition, I was able to switch my personality. Let's face it, you cannot change your real self. Be natural be authentic and people will love you.

This is a gradual process, this is something which I help you with in my mentorship. Do join if you want to become a powerful and fearless speaker.

Always be the first-best version of yourself, instead of the second-best version of somebody else. Judy Garland

MYTH #3. EXPERIENCED SPEAKERS DON'T GET NERVOUS

> ***"Mark Twain famously said, "There are two types of speakers in the world: the nervous and the liars.""***

Even experienced speakers face anxiety, but they have mastered the art of managing it. And guess what? After the first three to four minutes, you become comfortable with your audience and your nervousness decreases. We must realise that it is a human emotion and just continue making an excellent presentation.

MYTH #4. I HAVE TO MEMORIZE THE SPEECH

Well, you don't have to "memorize" you have to "internalise". It may have happened to you that when you try to memorise certain things, you tend to become tense or feel under pressure as a result you get blank, which makes it challenging for you to talk confidently and fearlessly on stage. Here's what you need to do: internalise your speech and make it a part of who you are.

> ***"Here are three things to aim at in public speaking: first, to get into your subject, then to get your subject into yourself, and lastly, to get your subject into the heart of your audience ~ Alexander Gregg"***

MYTH #5. YOU HAVE TO USE FANCY VOCABULARY

You don't need fancy/difficult words to sound intelligent. In fact, the simpler your language, the better you connect with the audience. It's possible that your audience doesn't understand what you're saying. You may have a diverse group of listeners, and it's your job to make each one feel included. By using fancy words you might sound intelligent but your purpose won't be achieved.

Know your audience and accordingly choose the best vocabulary.

MYTH #6. YOU HAVE TO ENTERTAIN THE AUDIENCE

As a public speaker, your purpose is to convey your message, not to entertain the audience. Focus on delivering a clear and engaging message that resonates with your audience.

YES, entertaining the audience is important so that your audience will be hooked towards you, but it is NOT a must.

MYTH #7. PEOPLE MIGHT LAUGH AT ME

Maybe! Maybe they won't! Okay, let's assume that they will. Laugh with them.

Laugh at yourself, have fun and remember this you are still alive. Get up, dust yourself and gear up for the next speech. It can't get worse than this.

MYTH #8. YOU HAVE TO BE AN EXPERT

Speaking to people is not about being an expert on matters. Just speak about what you know. You can still deliver a compelling speech by sharing your experiences, insights, and perspective.

You don't have to be the authority on everything. As long as you make sense, the listeners will be okay.

MYTH #9. YOU SHOULD SPEAK IN THE MIRROR TO PRACTICE

Let me tell you a story. You are sitting in an art class and drawing a sketch. Your teacher stands behind you looking over your work. Are you likely to make mistakes in such a scenario? Very likely!

And why is that?

When we know we are being evaluated, we are more likely to make mistakes.

When you look in the mirror and practice speaking, you are also constantly evaluating yourself – your voice, your expressions, and your body language. And this is going to be very distracting.

You never see yourself on the stage, the audience does. So looking at yourself in the mirror will only distract you from becoming better.

Remember, public speaking is a skill that can be learned and improved with practice, and these myths can limit your potential as a speaker. Don't let them hold you back.

CHALLENGE FOR YOU

1. Which of these myths were stopping you to present confidently & fearlessly from the stage?

____

____

____

____

____

2. Work on dispelling the myths that are preventing you from presenting confidently on stage.

____

____

CHAPTER FOUR

QUICK TIPS TO BECOME A MAGNETIC PUBLIC SPEAKER

Mastering the art of speaking can be a total game-changer for your business...and can accelerate your success. Simply sharing your experiences or insights with others can lead to more income, influence, and impact than you might think.

But it's not always easy to make a lasting impression when you're speaking in front of a crowd...including online and in-person... especially if you don't know how to use your voice and message to their full potential.

Here I will share with you, quick tips that will help you to become a magnetic public speaker.

1. NERVOUSNESS IS NORMAL

> ***"“Being a little nervous when you present means that you really care about what you have to say. Audience members see this as a signal that you care about earning their respect—there is a graceful humility here—and that you care enough to want to do a great job. Caring for your audience almost always has a boomerang effect.”— Bruna Martinuzzi"***

Everyone gets nervous before or while giving a presentation and it's pretty normal. Some nerves are healthy, but if you can feel your heart racing, inhale through your nose for 5 seconds and exhale from your mouth for 5 seconds. Just do this 10 times before your presentation to stabilise your heart rate.

2. KNOW YOUR AUDIENCE

Prior to anything else, you must have a clear understanding of your target audience. Research the demographic, background, and interests of your audience, and tailor your message to meet their needs and expectations. This will be covered in detail in a later chapter.

> ***"If you want to create messages that resonate with your audience, you need to know what they care about.- Nate Elliot"***

Blanco

3. START POWERFUL

Capture the audience's attention from the beginning with an engaging introduction or hook. In the first 15 seconds, your audience decides whether or not to pay attention to you, thus you must direct their attention to you right away. If you fail to grab their attention, you will fail to achieve your presentation goal.

There are various techniques to get your audience's attention, including using quotes, asking questions, telling stories, providing examples, opening with a prop, revealing certain facts, and many others. Make sure your presentation has a powerful opening to capture the attention of the audience right away.

4. BE PREPARED

> " ***"Before anything else, preparation is the key to success." – Alexander Graham Bell*** "

Prepare your presentation till the time you completely internalized it. Make your presentation part of you. Include examples, facts, stories, questions, and quotes to make your presentation even more powerful. After creating the structure of your presentation, present it out loud. Don't just practice it in your head, but practice it in front of people. And trust me you will WOW your audience.

5. USE STORYTELLING

> " ***"If you don't use stories audience members may enjoy your speech, but there is no chance they'll remember it."– Andrii Sedniev*** "

Storytelling stimulates our brain, as we connect with the message, we not only absorb the information but feel the emotions too. Storytelling has been part of our lives since childhood, and we love to listen to it. When we are sharing stories with our audience they get hypnotised towards us. Use stories to illustrate your points and make them more memorable and relatable to your audience.

6. USE INFLUENTIAL BODY LANGUAGE

> ***"People need realness, reality. People can sense when someone is being pretentious or fake. It's because you feel it; you see it in someone's body language. -Afrojack "***

Use confident, open, and engaging body language to connect with your audience and convey your message effectively. Public speaking is a whole-body affair. It means that every part of your body, from head to toe, is engaged when you speak in public. You might be wondering which body parts are engaged when giving a speech in public. Your head, eyes, mouth, tongue, ear, hands, shoulder, and legs are all used. By using these body parts, you captivate your audience and project the image of a magnetic speaker.

7. VARY YOUR DELIVERY

Vary the pace, tone, and volume of your delivery to keep the audience engaged and prevent boredom. Sometimes we tend to speak in a monotone manner that is uninteresting for our audience to hear. Because of this, we must use voice modulation to tempt our audience to listen to us from beginning to end.

> *"The words are their thoughts, the tone is their feelings- Darlene A. Austin"*

8. PRACTICE ACTIVE LISTENING

Pay attention to your audience's reactions and adjust your delivery as needed to keep their attention and connect with them. You've probably seen it happen occasionally, while you're giving a presentation, your audience is yawning or exhausted from listening to the speakers one after another. At that point, you need to hear the mood of your audience. If they are exhausted conduct some activities so they will refresh their mind. If you don't hear your audience, your audience won't hear you.

These tips are just the tip of the iceberg, you will learn a lot in upcoming chapters but by following these quick tips, you can give effective and engaging presentations that connect with your audience to achieve your presentation goals.

CHALLENGE FOR YOU

1. Practice your presentation by using your whole body(body language practice)
2. Put your presentation into practice by speaking it out loud.

CHAPTER FIVE

BLUNDERS TO AVOID IN PUBLIC SPEAKING

Are you ready to become a powerful public speaker? Of course, you are! You're here for a reason.

I like to consider mistakes as opportunities for learning and teaching. We learn from experiences. The following errors are the most frequent ones I've seen in my many years as a public speaking coach, and observer—and they're also the ones that are the simplest to fix.

Here are some common mistakes to avoid in public speaking to WOW your audience.

MISTAKE 1: RELYING TOO HEAVILY ON SLIDES

Over-reliance on slides can distract you from the delivery of your message and make the presentation dull. I recall the first presentation I made in 2018 for college students. I tried to include everything I could so I wouldn't forget anything. Guess what, your audience is there to hear you speak and learn from you, not to hear you read your slides. We often have the thought, "What if I forget?" and as a result, we rely heavily on slides. Stop this immediately; it prevents you from making a captivating presentation.

MISTAKE 2: FOCUSING TOO MUCH ON CONTENT AND NOT ENOUGH ON DELIVERY

While it's important to have a well-structured presentation, it's equally important to focus on your delivery and engage your audience.

Always have clarity in your mind deciding when to pause, when to ask your audience a question, when to conduct an activity, when to use stories, when to use quotes, when to modulate your voice, and when to include humour. This can be learned through practice, so please pay attention to how you deliver your message.

> "***"Speech is power. Speech is to persuade, to convert, to compel. – Ralph Waldo Emerson***"

MISTAKE 3: RELYING ON FILLER WORDS

These are those "you knows", so, like and ah's that we often use. In public speaking, using these filler words reduces the effect of the message and reveals nervousness or inexperience. How can you get rid of filler words?

It's simple, Just replace the fillers with a pause every time one pops up in your mind. Just practice it.

MISTAKE 4: STANDING BEHIND A PODIUM/LECTERN

When you stand behind a physical object such as a desk or lectern, you'll be creating a barrier between yourself and your audience. You'll find it much harder to connect authentically, you'll limit the natural hand & body gestures that can add character to your presentation, and you look less confident. Please avoid sanding behind the podium next time.

MISTAKE 5: LACK OF FACIAL EXPRESSION

You must use your facial expressions to connect with your audience and convey your message while giving a presentation. Unfortunately, we tend to stiffen our neck, facial and jaw muscles when we're anxious. We might appear expressionless and blank as a result we lack an emotional bond with our audience.

Here is the tip to follow to avoid stress expressions and to get confident expressions. You have to relax your facial muscles by doing quick face exercises. This is one of the techniques which I teach people in my public speaking mentorship.

MISTAKE 6: AVOIDING EYE CONTACT

When you're anxious, avoiding eye contact and staring at the floor or ceiling may seem like a great coping technique. When you do this your audience gets disconnected from you.

But I understand the moment you look right into your audience's eyes you get blank. Here the question arises, how to handle it? It's simple, just look at their eyebrows. Here your eyes and your eyebrows are nearer to each other. When you look at their eyebrows your audience feels you are looking at them. Try doing this activity with your siblings or friend.

MISTAKE 7: MISMANAGING TIME

As you prepare, keep a timer. Whether it's a meeting, on-stage presentation or a virtual session, going over time is an avoidable mistake. There are times when you are expected to give a presentation for an hour, but for whatever reason, you are only granted 30 minutes. In this case, you have to exclude some points from your presentation, but in the opposite case, you have to include additional examples and anecdotes or you can engage your audience in activities.

> ***"*"All we have to decide is what to do with the time that is given us" -J R. R.Tolkien*"**

Avoiding these common mistakes will help you deliver a confident and engaging presentation that connects with your audience. Don't worry too much if you recognise yourself in any of these errors. Each is relatively easy to fix and just takes some efforts and practice.

CHALLENGE FOR YOU

1. In your presentation, what blunders are you making?

____

____

____

____

2. Make a recording of your presentation on your smartphone and listen to it to identify fillers.

____

____

____

____

____

CHAPTER SIX

DISCOVER QUESTIONS TO KNOW YOUR AUDIENCE

You need to know your audience before giving a presentation because whatever you are presenting, should resonate with your audience. For example, The presentation you will provide for corporate executives and business leaders will be different from the one you will prepare for the school-going students.

> “***“Designing a presentation without an audience in mind is like writing a love letter and addressing it: To Whom It May Concern.” – Ken Haemer***”

You should therefore be aware of your target audience while making a presentation. Every time I have to make a presentation or speech, I inquire about the audience by asking the following questions to the organizer.

1. Who is my audience?
2. What is their age?
3. What is their level of understanding?
4. What is their profession?
5. Which language do they speak or understand?
6. What is their location?
7. Is it the general public or experts in your field?
8. What is the size of the audience?
9. If needed, their average income.
10. Do they think with their heart or their head?
11. What are their expectations?
12. What problems are they facing?

Once I get to know my audience, I create my presentation as per their needs. I use the example as per the audience. I use stories that can resonate with them and that they can relate to. That's how the presentation becomes more powerful, and I would encourage you to follow this list to know your audience and create your presentation.

CHALLENGE FOR YOU

1. Identify your audience and write down the answers to all the questions which you will ask the organiser before creating a presentation.

____

____

____

____

CHAPTER SEVEN

3 STEPS TO EXECUTE BEFORE PRESENTATION

Whenever you give a presentation, you need to keep in mind these three steps and then you need to give a presentation.

STEP 1: CREATE GPS FOR YOUR PRESENTATION

I remember the time when I used to face this problem when it comes to creating the presentation. I would get confused that, Where should I start? Should I gather more information, do more research, and study more about my presentation? Here you will get a clear idea about, the essential steps you need to take before creating a presentation.

Let's talk about that.

Before creating your presentation, you need to ask this question to yourself.

"What is the one thing, I want my audience to do after I have communicated with them?"

What result do you want from your audience?

You want them to work with you, or to invest in your company, you want them to give you a job, What do you want them to do after you communicated with them?

Take out a pen and paper and write down,

What is your goal for the presentation?

More specific will be better.

> ***"“Setting goals is the first step in turning the invisible into the visible.” – Tony Robbins"***

STEP 2: BRAINSTORM YOUR IDEAS

Once you identify your GOAL, BRAINSTORM. Brainstorm all the ideas which you have inside your mind.

Identify, what will motivate your audience to take action. It might be educating them, motivating them, or showing social proof. You need to understand, it is not about giving them all the information. It is about motivating them to do certain work. Brainstorm, which message will motivate your listener, to do what you want them to do.

Take pen and paper and write down all the ideas which you have inside your mind. It might be 10,20,30,40 or 50 write down all the ideas. After writing your ideas you will realize all the ideas are interconnected. I want you to create the top 5 points and sub-points of the interconnected idea.

For Example Point 1 - Subpoint 1, Subpoint 2, Subpoint 3.....

Point 5 - Subpoint 1, Subpoint 2, Subpoint 3

Communicate the top 5 messages because they are going to remember only five. People don't remember more than five points.

What are your 5 ideas which you want to communicate?

1. ____
2. ____
3. ____
4. ____
5. ____

STEP 3: USE STORIES TO CONVEY EVERY POINT

Use stories to convey every point to your audience. As Human beings, we are hardwired to listen to stories, We remember them for a longer period.

If it is possible, use a personal life story. Everyone's life is unique. The secret is people love personal life stories. You hook your audience towards you. Just share your experience. It is the best way to convey your message, it will make them understand and remember it better. Always involved **emotions, dialogues, and wow factor in stories.**

> " ***"Tell your story with your whole heart."— Brené Brown*** "

Make sure to use these 3 steps before communicating & presenting.

CHALLENGE FOR YOU

1. What is your GOAL for the Presentation?

____

2. What are your best 5 ideas?

____

____

____

____

____

3. Why according to you using stories are important?

____

____

____

CHAPTER EIGHT

MESMERIZE THE AUDIENCE THROUGH STORYTELLING

Storytelling is the key to success in presentations. While stories attract people of all ages. Good storytelling abilities are highly appreciated and people who can tell good stories are also loved by the audience.

> " ***"Trying to influence people by using words to appeal to their intellect isn't enough, We need stories." - Dr. Paul Homoly."*** "

Here are some tips to attract audiences through storytelling.

1. KEEP YOUR VISION CLEAR

Before creating any story you must decide what point you want to make or what message you want to convey. Keep your eye on the goal while creating your story. Ask yourself if it is helping you in achieving your goal; if not, change the approach and rewrite your story.

> ***"The one thing that you have that nobody else has is you. Your voice, your mind, your story, your vision. So write and draw and build and play and dance and live as only you can. -Neil Gaiman"***

2. FIND A RELATABLE STORY

Choose a story that is relevant to your audience and will resonate with them. For example, When you are telling a story to a child, you will take a different approach; you will connect the story to the child so that the child will understand it. Likewise, when you are telling a story to a professional, you will create a story that resonates with them; you will use examples that are suitable for their profession; and you will consider their level of understanding so that it will be highly relatable with your audience and help you influence and make an impact.

3. CREATE AN EMOTIONAL CONNECTION

Emotion is the key to engagement; make sure your audiences care about your story. Use storytelling to create an emotional connection with your audience by sharing experiences, feelings, and emotions. When you get your audience's attention then you can influence them to action.

> **"*"Good stories surprise us. They make us think and feel. They stick in our minds and help us remember ideas and concepts in a way that a PowerPoint crammed with bar graphs never can."*
> *-Joe Lazauskas* "**

4. USE BODY LANGUAGE

To improve and bring life to your story, use reasonable body language and gestures. This helps your audience visualize.

Make your audience feel like they were there by acting out key moments from your story instead of just telling them what happened. Also add some memorable elements such as humour, suspense, or surprise to keep your audience engaged.

5. CALL TO ACTION

Call to action means what action you want your audience to take after listening to your story. A compelling story will motivate & influence its audience to act. Design a story around a call to action that requires the storyteller to make it obvious what the next step is and to make it easy and obvious for your audience to take this next step.

By using these storytelling techniques, you can captivate your audience, create an emotional connection, and deliver your message more effectively.

CHALLENGE FOR YOU

1. What is the story's intended purpose, according to you?

____

____

____

2. What action do you want your audience to take after listening to you?

____

____

____

3. Practice storytelling by using body language.

CHAPTER NINE

STRUCTURE PERSUASIVE CONTENT

> "*Content isn't King, it's the Kingdom. -Lee Odden*"

The idea of giving a presentation can be intimidating and cause a lot of anxiety for many people. However, if you take some time to understand how effective presentations are structured and then apply this structure to your own presentation, you'll appear much more confident and relaxed.

Most people have lots of content with them, but this is not enough. You need to have quality content with the right structure.

Whenever you have to create presentation, divide your presentation by using **BME formula**

1. Beginning

2. Middle
3. End

1. BEGINNING

In the beginning, you need to create curiosity in the mind of your audience to get the attention of your listener. Understand, attention comes from curiosity. Here are some ways to create curiosity.

1. Ask them questions.
2. Use Props.
3. Quotes
4. Personal Life Stories.
5. Example
6. Joke
7. Complement your Audience.
8. Facts
9. Make them do an Activity
10. Long Pause
11. Make them Visualize
12. Hit their pain point

Introduce yourself

After creating curiosity give a quick introduction about yourself, for example, This is Author Nayan Chaudhary, I am international public speaking mentor and CEO of ANC transformation. To date, I have trained over 15,000 corporate professionals and business leaders from over 50 countries to speak confidently and fearlessly from the stage.

I am not going into details here, but I am creating authority and credibility through my introduction

Introduce your presentation

You must engage the interest and confidence of the audience in the introduction by outlining the topic and goal of your presentation. Touch your audience's pain point by stating the issues/challenges they are facing in their life.

2. MIDDLE

In middle, you need to share certain points, which will help them to remember. In the presentation, I've seen people give a lot of points to their audience, I want you to stop this. You need to give a minimum of three points and a maximum of 5 pointers, which clears your topic. I have observed in my life that whenever I give more than 5 points to people they couldn't remember it. They get overwhelmed by it. So in the middle part, you need to provide them with pointers.

For Example:

Topic:-Unleash your confidence and become an Unstoppable speaker

1. Conquer the fear of failure
2. Conquered the fear of judgement
3. Conquer the fear of success

Note: The main body of your talk needs to meet the promises you made in the introduction.

3. END

Your END decides, how much impact will you create on your listener. That's why your END should be on a high note. Here, you need to make your audience revise all the learnings which they have learned or that they need to focus on.

You have to end your presentation the way you started your presentation. As I've already mentioned, you should utilise the same tactics you used to start your presentation to finish it.

A presentation needs to be well-structured so it can have the most impact on your audience. Please avoid overloading it with too much information, and rehearse it several times to improve your delivery.

CHALLENGE FOR YOU

1. How can you start your presentation with a bang by arousing interest?

____

____

2. What tips will you provide in the middle of your presentation?

____

____

____

____

3. How will you wrap up your presentation?

____

____

CHAPTER TEN

WRONG WAY TO START YOUR PRESENTATION

Most of us have experienced dull, irrelevant or confusing presentations. But recall the most impressive presentation you recently witnessed.– one that was informative, motivating and inspiring. Don't you wish you could deliver presentations like that?

If you want to give a persuasive presentation, then please stop making this error when you begin your presentation. If you do, your audience won't take you seriously, won't pay attention to you, and won't do anything after you finish.

1. STARTING THE PRESENTATION BY NOT CREATING ENOUGH CURIOSITY

You must create curiosity in the beginning. You should know that your audience won't be compelled to listen to you from beginning to end unless and until you exhibit significant curiosity. In this book, I have already shown you how to create curiosity in a beginning, please refer to it.

2. INTRODUCING YOURSELF AT THE BEGINNING

People typically start their presentations by introducing themselves but keep in mind that others are listening to you for their own benefit and are interested in what precisely they will learn from you. What advantages they'll get from your speech?

First, tell people what benefits they are going to get from your presentation, and what kind of impact your presentation will have on their lives, and then you can introduce yourself. If you do so your audience will be more inclined to listen to you.

3. STARTING A PRESENTATION IN A BORING WAY

I've heard presenters introduce themselves or start a presentation by saying good morning to the audience, which is a dull approach to starting a presentation. Instead, you should grab the audience's attention within the first 15 seconds.

4. STARTING PRESENTATION BY READING SLIDES

Sometimes we over-write presentations because we are afraid of forgetting something. But keep in mind that when you're making a presentation, your audience should pay attention to you, not just to the slides. When you write too many things, your audience tends to read everything, and your audience's focus goes from you to the slides.

To create slides, follow these steps.

Every slide should consist of one word or one sentence with a picture. This will help your audience to visualize properly.

> "***"Through the picture, I see reality. Through the word, I understand it." – Sven Lidman***"

5. TELLING YOUR AUDIENCE THAT "I AM NERVOUS"

As soon as you say **"I am nervous,"** your audience starts to doubt your authority and credibility, which lowers their level of trust in you.

Please avoid making these mistakes in your presentation if you find yourself doing so. It makes your presentation dull and unattractive. Most importantly, the audience becomes bored and disinterested.

CHALLENGE FOR YOU

1. Which incorrect presentation technique are you using to begin your speech?

   ____

   ____

CHAPTER ELEVEN

START YOUR PRESENTATION POWERFULLY

In today's business, giving presentations to audiences of all sizes is quite common. Various professionals may be required to give specific presentations, such as a sales pitch, new marketing data presentation or analytical research results.

Regardless of the content, When it comes to engaging your audience, the presentation's opening may make or break it. There are many ways to start a presentation that will engage the hearts and minds of the people you want to convey your message to.

> “*"The beginning is the most important part of the work." -Plato*”

1. SHARING YOUR PERSONAL LIFE EXAMPLE

Giving a real-life example from your own experience can fascinate your audience and inspire them to stay attentive throughout your speech. They will be more likely to listen to you because you are here sharing a personal example or experience from your own life.

Follow a story hook that includes a main character, an obstacle or challenge related to the presentation topic, a description of how that obstacle or challenge was overcame, and a summary of the lessons the protagonist gained that may be applied to the audience.

2. HOOK YOUR AUDIENCE WITH A BOLD STATEMENT

If you don't have a personal story to share with the audience, consider sharing a thought-provoking fact about your presentation's relevance. If you decide to go forward with this approach, make sure to deliver your statement with confident body language and persuasive verbal tone.

EXERCISE: Stand up straight and keep your hands out of your pockets. Make an open gesture to make yourself appear authoritative and credible. By doing this, you provide the impression to your audience that what you are saying is both truthful and interesting.

3. ASK FOR AUDIENCE PARTICIPATION

If you do not plan to make a bold statement or tell a story, ask your audience to participate. The best way to do this is by asking an open-ended question that requires them to either raise a hand or stand up to answer. If it is early in the morning, try asking them to stand up when they answer your question. This advice works best in more intimate to small-scale audiences.

4. USING PROPS

What are props? Props are objects that can be used to project something. Props might be anything from a cell phone to a pen to a bottle & cloth. You may utilise whatever material you see around you as a prop. However, be certain that it relates to your subject. This will create curiosity in your audience's mind to listen to you carefully.

5. THE POWER OF SILENCE

What would you do if you attended a presentation where the speaker started the presentation but then remained silent for the first 30 seconds? Here you are expecting the orator to speak but the speaker is not speaking anything. The speaker's silence draws the audience's attention to him or her because this is not what they would normally expect. Most likely, your audience's mind starts racing with thoughts, expecting something of vital importance to be disclosed. Use the power of silence at the beginning of your presentation to hook your audience towards you.

6. TELL A JOKE

Tell a joke to get the audience to laugh. This can be a technique to lighten the room and establish a stronger connection with the audience, even for experts. Don't overdo it because it could distract people from your goal, but when used correctly, this strategy can be a powerful way to start any presentation.

7. QUOTE AN INFLUENTIAL PERSON

One of the easiest ways to start a presentation is to quote an influential person. In these cases, it's best to use a concise, short and relevant quote to catch your audience's attention. If you are using slides, include a photo of the person you are quoting to give your presentation more depth and character.

Use the tactics I've just shared with you if you desire to make a strong first impression on your audience and keep them interested in you during your presentation. These strategies will make sure that they are drawn to you.

CHALLENGE FOR YOU

1. Why, in your opinion, is it crucial to capture your audience's attention in the beginning?

____

____

____

2. At the start, how will you grab the attention of your audience?

____

____

____

3. To grab your audience's attention, which of the strategies discussed above will you use?

____

____

CHAPTER TWELVE

END THE PRESENTATION ON A HIGH NOTE

How you end a presentation is just as important as how you start it. A weak ending will leave them bored and uninspired, within a few hours they may even have forgotten your message. But a strong ending will fire them up and also motivates and empowers them. A strong ending encourages people to take action. So how do you end on a high? Here are 5 tips to ensure you go out with a bang.

1. CALL YOUR AUDIENCE TO ACTION

It's not enough to assume your message will inspire people to take action. You need to tell them to take action. An excellent method to end is to summarise the action you want your listeners to take. For that use these 2 approach:

Start with a negative motivation – help them see how bad things will be if they don't do what you are suggesting.

Finish with a positive motivation – paint a picture of how great things will be when they do what you recommend."

Always give the negative first, followed by the positive. You'll leave the audience feeling inspired and increase your chances of moving them to action.

2. END YOUR PRESENTATION THE WAY YOU STARTED

You are aware of exactly how to begin your presentation since we covered it in great detail in the previous chapter. You can use those techniques to successfully conclude your presentation as well.

For example, At the start of your presentation, you included a quote. You can use the quote to conclude your presentation. It may be the same or different, but it must be relevant to the subject. Additionally, you can start your speech with a question, and then respond to it at the end.

3. END WITH A SUMMARY

> “*"If you've already explained your content well and in an engaging way, there is no need to summarize the content again at the end," -Dee Clayton* ”

There are far more powerful ways to end your presentation. However, it might be necessary if your message is particularly complicated or your speech is a long one.

Summarizing content can be a little dry – both for you and your audience. Make your summary more enjoyable with humour, and a fascinating anecdote. The best way is to ask your audience their top three learnings from the presentation.

4. DON'T END BY ANSWERING QUESTIONS

We frequently think that by answering questions from the audience, we can wrap up our presentation. But NO. When you're done, include a call to action. If time permits, address questions from the audience.

> “*"Never end with the questions. Too many people make this mistake. If you get a negative question, you've dulled the whole presentation and the audience leave on a negative note. Always do the questions before the wrap up." -Dee Clayton*”

Too many people end with questions and it often goes off track. This is memorable for no one. By the time you've answered a handful of semi-relevant questions, the audience have forgotten most of what you've told them.

5. THANK YOUR AUDIENCE

Before you go, remember to always thank your audience. After all, they've stayed until the end, right? Show gratitude to the audience for their time and attention, and express your appreciation for their interest in your topic. Here is what I say to my audience to thank them

Thank you so much for being here till the end, it shows how committed and inclined you are for your growth and transformation.

Discover/create a phrase which resonates with your topic.

Your presentation needs to be concluded in such a way that it reinforces your message, leaves a positive impression, and ensures that your audience leaves with a positive experience.

CHALLENGE FOR YOU

1. How will you wrap up your next presentation?

____

____

____

2. Make a closing statement thanking your audience.

____

____

____

3. How will you use both negative and positive motivation to persuade your audience to act?

____

____

____

____

____

____

CHAPTER THIRTEEN

BOOST YOUR SELF-ESTEEM & CONFIDENCE TO BECOME AN UNSTOPPABLE SPEAKER

> *"The most beautiful thing you can wear is confidence." — Blake Lively*

Even if you are familiar with all the tactics for public speaking, they won't help if you lack the self-confidence to speak up in front of others. To become an unstoppable speaker, you must increase your self-worth and confidence.

Here the question arises, **What is self-esteem?**

Self-esteem is the reputation which you have about yourself.

If you want to achieve all of your goals and turn your dreams into reality, you must have a high level of self-esteem and confidence since these qualities enable you to maintain faith in yourself.

Let's discuss how you may raise these levels...

1. WRITE DOWN YOUR ALL WINS FROM CHILDHOOD

Every time a traumatic event occurs in life, we begin to lose confidence in ourselves, and at that point, we must reflect on all of our accomplishments.

Give a challenge to yourself, and list at least 30 of your accomplishments from childhood. The more you write, the better.

2. MAKE A COMMITMENT & FULFIL IT.

Sometimes we make commitments to ourselves that we don't keep. Whenever we make a commitment and when we break it, we are telling our mind that we are lying, and as a result, that belief steadily grows and lowers our confidence and self-esteem. Here, don't overcommit to yourself; instead, create tiny commitments that you are guaranteed to fulfil. This will send a message to your mind that no matter what happens, you will achieve it.

Here is a challenge for you make one commitment to yourself today and accomplish it today itself.

3. CREATE A JOURNAL

Journaling is the best way to reflect on our life. It helps me incredibly. All you have to do is just,

Write down

1. What went well in a day?
2. What I can improve?
3. Write your 3 Successes of the day.

This help me to boost my confidence level and I am following this for the last 5 years, I would encourage you to do the same.

4. CONFIDENCE COMES FROM TAKING ACTION

You cannot replace action with anything, and the more action you take, the more confident you will become. When you take certain actions, two things can happen:

1. Either you succeed or
2. You learn from your experiences.

As a result, when you take action, you discover what works and what does not, and you can then work on the things that work to achieve amazing results in your life. "Something is better than doing nothing".

> " ***"Don't wait until everything is just right. It will never be perfect...Get started now. With each step you take, you will grow stronger and stronger, more and more skilled, more and more***

self-confident, and more and more successful." - —Mark Victor Hansen"

5. SPEAK POSITIVELY ABOUT YOURSELF

Always talk positively about yourself. Would you want to be friends with someone who only speaks negatively about you? No, right?

Good friends always want you to succeed and will always positively interact with you. Make yourself your best friend and encourage yourself, empower yourself, and keep learning new things for positivity.

> ***""We must have perseverance and above all confidence in ourselves. We must believe that we are gifted for something and that this thing must be attained." —Marie Curie"***

6. PRIORITIZE ACTION OVER FEELINGS

Sometimes we procrastinate taking action. After all, we don't feel like doing it. This lowers our confidence and self-esteem because we prioritise our feelings over our actions. However, when you start acting, you will inevitably start having feelings, so if something is important to you, act on it, and feelings will follow.

7. CONFIDENCE COMES FROM LIFE LONG LEARNING ATTITUDE

Do you feel more confident when you learn something new? Of course, you do, and that's what happens when you continue to learn new things and skills. This doesn't mean that you have to learn only about your area of expertise; you can learn about any skill that piques your interest. However, by continuing to learn, you give your life meaning and feel empowered and confident.

8. CHANGE YOUR PHYSIOLOGY

Let's engage in the activity.

Lower your shoulders, cross your legs, cross your arms, and observe yourself. How are you feeling? Not so confident? Isn't it?

On the other hand, maintain a straight posture while standing or sitting, opening your arms and legs as you do so. Observe, how are you feeling? You must be feeling confident. Always keep your body open, it gives a signal to your brain that you are in a safe zone and it helps you to feel confident and relaxed.

I would strongly urge you to put all of the tactics I've provided you here into practice because I've done it in my own life and have assisted thousands of mentees in doing the same. They all have a proven track record, so please implement it.

CHALLENGE FOR YOU

1. Grab a piece of paper and list all of your achievements going back to childhood—minimum 30, maximum no limit—and stick it to the wall of your bedroom. (Start your day by reading your achievements).

2. Make a commitment(task) to yourself that you will keep today(Write down).

____

____

3. What step will you take this month/week to improve your confidence or what weaknesses have been holding you back for a long time?

____

____

____

CHAPTER FOURTEEN

AFFIRMATION TO BOOST YOUR CONFIDENCE BEFORE PRESENTATION

Right before giving the presentation, there are various inner dialogues that go on in the mind of the speaker. It might be positive or negative.

But if we want to give a great presentation, we need to have the right inner dialogues. I will provide you with the affirmation that I use before giving a presentation, and you can also use the same to have a great attitude before presenting

1. I am a super confident person.
2. I love my audience, and my audience loves me.
3. I am going to give a great presentation.
4. I have massive value to deliver.

5. I can make a difference.
6. People will get massive value from my presentation.
7. My audience is eager to hear what I have to say.
8. This will skyrocket my growth both personally and professionally.
9. People here will love what I have to say.
10. I am deserving of success and recognition for my efforts.
11. I have the knowledge and expertise to deliver a great presentation.
12. I trust in my abilities and I am ready to shine.
13. I am capable of delivering a powerful and impactful message.
14. I am excited to share my ideas and connect with my audience.
15. I am unstoppable.

Please use these affirmations aloud before performing on stage, so that you will experience tremendous self-confidence.

CHALLENGE FOR YOU

1. Please say aloud the affirmations that are stated above. Feel the emotions, express them using your entire body, and share your experience in the space provided.

CHAPTER FIFTEEN

CONQUER THE FEAR OF JUDGEMENT

Predominantly people face stage fear because they think too much about what people may think of them. Let me ask you 1 question.

DO YOU GET NERVOUS ON STAGE, THINKING ABOUT WHAT PEOPLE MIGHT THINK OF YOU?

If YES?

Remember, What people think of you is NONE of your business. Also - people don't really think of you.

You cannot please everyone.

Let me share something that will blow your mind: no one thinks of you.

People are too busy thinking about themselves constantly.

Think of it this way, who do you think of all day long?

Who do you worry about? "**YOURSELF**"

And so does everybody else. Definitely, we think about the person for a split second when we witness them falling or acting strangely, but we quickly forget about them. You have absolutely NO REASON to be nervous and overly aware of what others think of you while presenting, as they simply don't.

How freeing is that?

Now, you might say, 'but Author Nayan, I feel like people don't like me or approve of how I look, what I do etc.'

Guess what -It's acceptable if other people don't like you. Not everybody has excellent taste; furthermore, everyone has a different belief system that makes them unique. Accept & move on!

Fear of judgment stops us to express ourselves confidently and fearlessly.

As a result, anytime we express ourselves publicly or in front of a group of people, we continuously worry that others will judge us, which causes us to become self-centric. We focus entirely on ourselves,

- How do I look?
- How am I presenting?
- What are my facial expressions?
- How is my behaviour?
- How does my body language look?

and a lot more. This disconnects the speaker from the audience.

Here are some activities we need to implement in our lives to conquer the fear of judgement.

1. ONLY FOCUS ON SERVING

Whenever you are presenting, focus only on helping people. Focus on how your presentation will add value to your audience's lives.

How will it change their lives? This helps you to stop thinking about people's judgements and you start serving, which creates an impact.

> ***“"It's hard to be nervous when your heart's on service." - Rory Vaden”***

2. LET PEOPLE JUDGE YOU

We don't want people to judge us, but what if we let people judge us? This helps you to conquer the fear of judgment. Because no matter what we do, there will be some people who judge. It's human nature. Always remember, as human beings, we are perfectly imperfect.

> ***“There is only one way to avoid criticism: do nothing, say nothing, and be nothing.- Elbert Mubba'rd”***

3. DO SOME ACTIVITIES TO LET PEOPLE JUDGE YOU

We need to let people continuously judge us by engaging in some activity if we want to overcome the judgmental sensation that exists within us.

Take singing in a garden as an example. You can sing there with any voice, whether it is melodic or not. You will initially feel incredibly uncomfortable if someone says something negative about you, but when you repeat it, you won't feel anything.

That is what happens when you are on stage, first because the fear of judgement makes you feel bad or uncomfortable, but after that, you will show yourself brilliantly because you overcame the fear of judgement.

I would encourage you to implement this.

CHALLENGE FOR YOU

1. What approach will you use to overcome your fear of being judged?

____

____

2. What actions will you take that will cause others to judge you? (3 activities per day)

____

____

____

CHAPTER SIXTEEN

RIGHT WAY TO PRACTICE PUBLIC SPEAKING

You've probably heard this "PRACTICE MAKES A MAN PERFECT," but in my opinion, **"RIGHT PRACTICE MAKES A MAN IMPROVE".**

Before discussing, what you should do during proper practice, let's discuss what you should avoid doing while honing your public speaking skills.

AVOID PRACTICING SPEECHES IN FRONT OF A MIRROR

While practising their presentations, people frequently make a few blunders. You must have been told this from your childhood to practice your speeches in front of a mirror, yet doing so is one of the worst mistakes that individuals do since it causes us to become self-centric.

While practising in front of a mirror, we often focus on our flaws, such as how we appear, how we behave, how we express ourselves, if we look silly, whether we make errors, or whether we stumble, which lowers our confidence. For this reason, you should never practice in front of a mirror.

Here the question arises how you are supposed to practice your presentation? What are the ways to practice your presentation? let's talk about that...

1. PRACTICE IN FRONT OF THE CAMERA

Nowadays everyone has a mobile phone. All you need to do is place your phone someplace, start recording, and talk into the camera. Once your speech or presentation has been recorded, you may analyze it. Simply pay attention to how you sound and if you are enjoying your speech or not, then keep practising until you are confident with it.

Next time whenever you have to give your presentation, don't practice your presentation in front of the mirror but practice by using your mobile phone.

2. PRACTICE IN FRONT OF YOUR LOVED ONES

Once you've rehearsed a presentation in front of the camera and became confident & comfortable, practice it in front of your family and friends. They might be your parents, siblings, coworkers, or anyone else. Practice your presentation in front of strangers after you feel at ease speaking in front of friends and family or other familiar faces.

3. PRACTICE ON THE TERRACE OR IN THE GARDEN

When others are around and you are giving a presentation there, you will feel uneasy since you don't know who is going to be listening to you and, of course, you will be afraid of being judged. Which we mostly possess while presenting. Practice in the garden or on the terrace in front of strangers if you want to. This will give you greater self-assurance and give you the strength and bravery to deliver a fantastic presentation.

4. PRACTICE BY VISUALIZING

Confidence always comes from evidence. You need to give a lot of evidence to yourself to feel confident from the inside. When it comes to public speaking, confidence is crucial. The question arises how will you give evidence to yourself to give a great presentation...

Believe me, you can still give a great presentation even though you have no experience in presenting or going on stage to present in front of a group of people or hundreds and thousands of audience.

All you have to do is to **Visualize YOURSELF SUCCEEDING IN THE PRESENTATION.**

Your mind can't differentiate between reality and imagination, and when you visualize that you are succeeding while giving a presentation, you tend to succeed.

1st situation:

Let's imagine that you are imagining in your mind that you are not doing well. You forgot your speech, you are getting nervous, and your audience is not enjoying it. Your audience is getting bored. The chances are it will happen in reality. But on the flip side,

2nd situation:

If you imagine that you are doing incredibly well, you are confident while presenting, you are expressing yourself with full of energy and enthusiasm, your audience is loving your presentation, and your audience is getting massive value through your presentation. When you imagine that your audience is changing their lives through your speech, you start to feel incredibly confident from the inside.

Remember, only visualization will not help you. You need to believe completely that it will happen. You have to visualise your success and you will convert your visualisation into reality because here your mind believes that you have given lots of presentations.

Next time when you give your presentation, make sure to visualise your success in your mind because confidence comes from evidence.

5. LEARN BY OBSERVING

Observing and listening are the initial steps in honing your public speaking abilities. I used to go to a lot of events where speakers from different fields would be speaking before I started my path into public speaking. Of course, the goal was to learn from speakers about their expertise and also watching, listening, and observing them.

Here are the things which I used to observe in the speakers...

1. I used to observe how they engage their audience.
2. How are they asking questions?
3. Which activities are they conducting?

4. If the audience is not responding, how are they handling it? How are they handling questions?
5. How they are playing with their voice or voice modulation?
6. How do they add humour to the speech or presentation?
7. What makes their speech interesting?
8. What motivates people to take action?
9. What kinds of stories and examples are they using to captivate the audience?
10. What makes the audience laugh?
11. What makes the audience offended?
12. What made the audience interested?

If you want to become an incredible speaker then you have to observe the speaker and the audience too. Next time when you will go and attend an online or offline workshop, make sure to observe the speaker and the audience, this will help you for your next speech or presentation. You can imitate whatever you like but in your unique style.

CHALLENGE FOR YOU

1. Practice your presentation in front of the camera and analyse it.

____

____

2. Take notes while you are listening to your favourite speaker so that you can use them in your presentation.

____

____

3. Visualise your presentation success in your mind.

CHAPTER SEVENTEEN

WHAT CAUSES PUBLIC SPEAKING FEAR?

Before jumping to the best way to conquer the fear of public speaking, let's understand where exactly the fear of public speaking comes from?

What is the root cause of this fear? Why do we have the fear of public speaking? Let's discuss that......

Here, I would like to share with you a story, thousands of years ago, we used to live in a jungle in a tribe... in order to survive, we would get everything from the tribe food, shelter, and protection. But what if due to some reasons, tribe members kicked you out of the tribe?

Then you would not get food. You would not get protection and shelter. You would be completely alone and, as a result, any wild animal could come to you, grab you, attack you, kill you and eat. So, at that time, being alone was equal to death.

That was the reason we were so terrified of being by ourselves and away from the group (tribe). Considering that our lives were in danger at the moment.

Similarly, when you are on stage, you are alone, and that's why you tend to feel nervous. You get sweat, you start shivering and you feel like going away from that place because you are alone and your audience is together.

But you need to understand that now you don't have the fear of losing your life, now people will not hit you people will not kill you, right? Since we are having this FEAR for so many years. That's why this fear is ingrained in us. All we have to do is face it and conquer it.

> ***"“Feel the fear of public speaking and do it anyway.” – Arvee Robinson"***

CHALLENGE FOR YOU

1. Why do you feel anxious on stage? Please explain in detail.

____

____

____

____

____

____

2. What feelings or thoughts do you have when you're anxious?

____

____

____

____

CHAPTER EIGHTEEN

DESTROY YOUR FEAR OF PUBLIC SPEAKING

> *"“According to most studies, people’s number one fear is public speaking. Number two is death. Death is number two. Does that sound right? This means to the average person, if you go to a funeral, you’re better off in the casket than delivering the eulogy.” – Jerry Seinfeld"*

Now let’s discuss the best way to conquer the fear of public speaking.

1. STOP PLEASING PEOPLE

Generally, when we present, we believe that the entire audience should love our presentation. Well, it is not true. Let’s understand this...

1st situation:

Whenever you get on stage, the majority of the audience will look at you and say, "The speaker looks reasonable." I hope I will learn something from the speaker. Here, their expectations are not too high or too low.

2nd situation:

Similarly, there will be some people in the audience who will look at you and say, "I don't know why, but I really like the speaker." I can resonate with the speaker, I really love whatever the speaker is presenting.

3rd situation:

But on the flip side, there will be some people in the audience who will look at you and say, "I don't know why, but I don't like the speaker." I couldn't resonate with the speaker.

So please stop people-pleasing. Understand everyone will not love your presentation because everyone has a different mindset, belief system, thought processes, and experiences. That's what makes each individual unique.

Once you understand that you cannot please everyone, you reduce your stress, worries, and anxiety. You feel extremely lite and you present yourself fearlessly and confidently.

2. CONVERT NERVOUSNESS INTO EXCITEMENT

Whenever you feel anxiety don't say to yourself that "I am feeling anxious and nervous". Just say to yourself that I am feeling excited. When you are excited and when you are nervous, the symptoms are the same. i.e Your heart beats increase, you start shivering, you start sweating.

Next time whenever you feel nervous, just say that I am excited... I am excited about the presentation and you shift your focus positively.

3. FOCUS ON PROVIDING VALUE

Do you get nervous or feel hesitation, while presenting on stage? YES? The solution is simple,

Focus on providing value. It's hard to get nervous when you are focusing on serving people. Focus on your listener, not on yourself.

You can be a bad speaker but still, you can present fearlessly.

Initially, you will be probably a bad speaker, who needs to be fearless.

So, how do you overcome your fear?

- It's not practice.
- It's not you.
- It's them.

It's about your audience!

Before the presentation, we often get these thoughts in our mind that....

- What if I'm not engaging and the audience gets bored?
- What if I don't know what to say?
- What if I forget what I have to say?
- What if people laugh at me?

Stop thinking of yourself!

- When you think of yourself, you get nervous.
- When you think of helping the audience, you feel empowered.

Great speakers know the secret of being fearless, it is focusing on helping the audience to get their desired results.

Next time when you're on a stage, just think :

- I will empower the crowd!
- I will provide massive value in my audience's life
- I will change their lives!
- My presentation will help my audience to get great results.

These thoughts don't make you nervous.

- These thoughts make you feel empowered.
- These thoughts give you purpose.

Overcoming your fear of speaking is the easy way of giving successful speeches. Change your focus. Conquer your fear.

4. YOUR AUDIENCE WANTS YOU TO PERFORM WELL

Your audience is always with you when you are performing on stage. They want to get value from you. They want to learn from you. They are not there to waste their time. Consider a scenario where you are attending a presentation or workshop. What exactly are you thinking in your head? Since you are there to learn, the speaker should deliver an effective speech.

But let's say that speaker messed up. Then you feel bad about it. You feel bad for the speaker because it might hamper their reputation. Understand your audience wants you to perform well.

5. TALK WITH YOUR AUDIENCE BEFORE PRESENTING

I would encourage you to talk with your audience before giving a presentation. This will help you to overcome the fear of the unknown.

We are unable to exhibit ourselves boldly and courageously because we are afraid of the unknown.

Here the question arises, what will you talk with your audience? What questions can you ask your audience?

1. Ask them where you are from.
2. Which language do you speak?
3. Which profession are you in?
4. What are your goals?
5. What do you expect from this presentation?
6. Where do you see yourself in 3 to 5 years?

When you interact with your audience, your audience will connect with you when you are presenting, and they will be the ones who engage with you the most.

CHALLENGE FOR YOU

1. Why you should stop pleasing people to become fearless?

____

____

____

____

2. What questions will you ask your audience before a presentation?

____

____

____

____

____

____

3. What mindset you should have before going on stage?

____

____

____

____

CHAPTER NINETEEN

GENERATE MONEY THROUGH PUBLIC SPEAKING SKILLS

One of the highest-paying careers in the world is public speaking, where speakers make thousands of dollars for short talks at events, conferences, and companies. Here's how to get started, even if you have zero experience giving talks.

1. SPEAK FOR FREE

If you've never given a talk before, how do you get booked? You speak for free. The reality is that it's far easier to get opportunities when you're already doing public speaking. Reach out to local schools, colleges and organizations or leverage your network to get in front of an audience, no matter how small. Speak for free on the subject of your expertise. Even if you're not getting paid (yet), these first gigs will give you credibility and experience you can convert into bigger and better opportunities.

2. SPEAK FOR A SMALL FEE

As you transition from free to paid, be willing to take a modest fee. Set your fee so you can get hired at least twice or three times each month, no matter where you are in your paid speaking career. This profession takes a lot of practice in front of live audiences. There is no replacement!

3. GRAB ALL SPEAKING OPPORTUNITIES

Before I started getting paid for speaking and training, I did tons of FREE events. I still do FREE speaking events. It helps me in increasing my visibility, obtaining numerous paid opportunities, and testing new content.

Moreover, it enables me to keep my speaking skills up-to-date. Public speaking is like a muscle. The more you exercise it, the stronger it gets. The more public speaking you do, the better you get at it. EVERY SINGLE SPEECH MATTERS!

4. OFFER KEYNOTE SPEECHES

This is what most people think of when they hear about making money through public speaking. Get speaking engagements at conferences and gatherings to deliver keynote speeches on topics that you are knowledgeable and passionate about.

5. SELL PRODUCTS OR SERVICES

Use your speaking engagements as an opportunity to promote and sell your products or services. Create your products and services as per your area of expertise. Promote your product whenever you get a speaking opportunity free or paid. Here is another piece of advice, if you have been invited to give a free speech, ask the event organizer if you can promote your services. This will be a win-win situation for both.

6. WRITE BOOKS OR CREATE ONLINE CONTENT

Use your knowledge and expertise to write books, create online courses, or produce other content that can generate income. If I talk about myself, I've authored three books so far, and along with them, I've created various courses on social communication, public speaking skills, and other topics as well. Develop and sell products like books, audio recordings, or video tutorials to help others improve their skills.

7. DIVERSIFY YOUR INCOME STREAMS

Consider creating multiple income streams from your public speaking skills, such as offering coaching, consulting, or speaking events. Take advantage of all the income streams, don't just depend on one.

It's crucial to remember that earning money through public speaking requires time, effort, and a strong dedication to constantly hone your abilities.

CHALLENGE FOR YOU

1. How will you begin offering free speaking engagements?

____

____

____

____

____

2. What products or services are you planning to produce to add an additional source of income?

____

____

____

____

____

CHAPTER TWENTY

GET SPEAKING OPPORTUNITIES ONLINE & OFFLINE

Participating in events and public speaking programs can be done in numerous ways. To do anything, we need to start taking small steps towards our goals. Remember that it will take time. In addition, we would lose faith, confidence, and the strength to keep going if we focus on taking massive steps and expecting results immediately.

Here, I will share with you some steps which you can take to achieve your goal of participating in online and offline events. Once you will start following these steps you don't need to look for an opportunity but the opportunities automatically come your way...

1. START CREATING VIDEOS

I know you want to speak in programs and events but if we will directly approach, then the chances are we would not get the opportunity to speak. Share your knowledge and experiences with others on the various social media platforms you have access to, and eventually, speaking engagements will present themselves to you.

2. BECOME AN EXPERT IN YOUR FIELD

To share anything, you need to have some area of expertise. That is when people will start trusting you. You will build your credibility and authority in your niche. In my case, my area of expertise is public speaking, social communication skills and mindset development. Figure out your area of expertise and start sharing your experiences with people in the form of video.

3. CREATE YOUR COMMUNITY

Why search for other audiences when you can create or have your own? Create a group on any social media platform and go live in it. There you can share your experiences and knowledge with other people. Also, you are doing your speaking practice before going to the bigger stage.

4. CONDUCT WEBINARS OR WORKSHOPS ONLINE

Once you develop your community, it becomes easy for you to conduct webinars or workshops online. People would love to listen to you because they are listening to you for a long time. Again you are not looking for others to give you opportunities but you are creating your own opportunities.

5. CONDUCT YOUR WORKSHOPS OFFLINE

When you have developed authority and credibility online, it becomes easy for you to gain trust, and you position yourself as an expert. As a result of all the information you have already provided online, when you offer offline workshops, people will come to learn, and you can take advantage of it.

6. GET OPPORTUNITIES

When people see you every day on different social media, automatically, people who organise events will invite you to speak at their events. This happened to me, I was working offline as well as online but the moment I started working online due to COVID, I started getting a lot of opportunities from different organisations both online and offline. It will happen to you as well.

7. GENERATE MONEY

Visibility = Money. The more visibility = more people know you & you will generate more money. We cannot pursue things in the long run if we are not generating money. It helps us to get more resources to help more people, and you generate money through your visibility. All you have to do is have more visibility. Attend networking events, approach people, talk with them, and speak at events for free or paid. Get in front of people.

If you really desire to pursue your public speaking career, then please make sure to follow these steps. If you're interested in becoming a public speaker but don't know where to start, you can get in touch with me and schedule a paid consultation call. I will share my years of experience with you and help you attain the results, which took me years to achieve.

CHALLENGE FOR YOU

1. What action are you going to take right now to grab opportunities both online and offline?

____

____

____

____

2. What is your action plan for creating more visibility?

____

____

____

____

____

____

Advanced Communication Skills, 12 Books In 1 (become Magnetic Speaker Now!)

Grab the Book Now!

Advanced Communication Skill is the most comprehensive book for you to live an Extra-Ordinary Life. If you want to grab this book, **it is available in both e-book & hard copy**. Please WhatsApp us at +91 9604901971 to grab.

After reading this book,

1. You will skyrocket your confidence level.
2. You will get rid of your Self-doubts and Insecurities for a Lifetime.
3. You could able to Earn more Money, more Fame, a Lavish Lifestyle & Massive Respect from Colleagues, Clients & Team Members.
4. You will destroy your fear.
5. You will able to handle difficult people easily.
6. You will get massive success in your personal and professional life.
7. You will able to approach, interact, connect and make an amazing first impression.
8. You will able to influence people.
9. You will get 360° of transformation in your life.

Level up your skills...

About The Author

Author Nayan Chaudhary (ANC)

Author Nayan Chaudhary Is A International Public Speaking Mentor, Founder & CEO of ANC Transformation. She helps Corporate professionals & Business Leaders to Master Public Speaking Skills, Winning Social Skills & to 10X their Revenue.

ANC also offers one-on-one consultations, group training, and large-scale workshop facilitation. She has trained over 15,000 corporate professionals and business leaders from more than 50 countries to date.

In addition, ANC is the author of various books, Advanced Communication Skills & Become Magnetic Public Speaker is 1 of them.

She also got featured on V4News, Global TV, V4Stream, and a variety of other news outlets. She's on a mission to help 1 million people to realize their true potential by mastering public speaking skills.

"Only Knowing things is not enough; we must apply it. Willing is not enough; we must implement it. Consistency is harder when nobody is clapping for you. You must clap for yourself during those times, you should always be Your Biggest Fan."

“"The Quality Of Your Life Is Based On Your Quality Decisions!" -Author Nayan Chaudhary”

Connect Us On Social Media For Your Transformation

YouTube: Author Nayan Chaudhary

Facebook page: Author Nayan Chaudhary

LinkedIn: Author Nayan Chaudhary

Instagram Id: author.nayan

WhatsApp: +91 96049-01971

9 798889 862048

Printed by Libri Plureos GmbH in Hamburg,
Germany